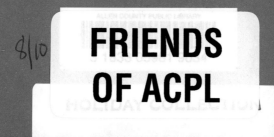

O Christmas Tree

Its History and Holiday Traditions

Jacqueline Farmer

Illustrated by **Joanne Friar**

ini Charlesbridge

glittering Christmas tree, trimmed for the holiday season, is a joyful sight. Children can't wait to decorate their trees for the holidays. Families love to see the decorations on their neighbors' trees. People come together to celebrate the tree lighting at the town hall. Christmas trees make us feel happy and uplifted.

How did the Christmas tree custom begin? The story goes back many centuries.

Evergreens are trees and bushes that remain green year-round. Lush branches from these plants have been used in holiday celebrations and ceremonies for more than three thousand years.

Around 1300 BCE, Egyptian families decorated their homes with palm branches to mark the winter solstice, the shortest day of the year. It was a happy holiday, for evergreens reminded the Egyptians that as the hours of daylight increased, their crops would begin to grow.

Ancient Romans also celebrated the winter solstice.
Their festival was called Saturnalia, in honor of Saturn,
the god of farming. Like the Egyptians, Romans brightened
up their homes with evergreen branches, knowing that
soon their crops would be flush with new green growth.

In the early days of the fifth century CE, many people in eastern Europe placed pine branches around the doors and windows of their homes. They hoped the branches would keep them safe from evil spirits.

This practice continued until the year 725 when, as the story goes, a missionary from Britain named Boniface arrived in Europe. One day he came upon a Germanic tribe at the sacred Oak of Donar. The people there were about to perform an animal sacrifice. To stop them, Boniface chopped down their sacred tree.

Boniface then pointed to a small, cone-laden fir tree sprouting nearby. He said the fir was a holy tree of the Christ Child; its triangular shape symbolized the Holy Trinity of Christianity, and its branches pointed toward heaven. Boniface urged the people to bring evergreen trees into their homes and to surround them with gifts for their families. He called these signs of love and kindness.

Legend says that the little tree at the Oak of Donar was the first tree with its roots in Christian teaching.

From the eleventh century to the end of the sixteenth century, plays based on Bible stories became popular. They were known as miracle plays. The most famous was the Paradise play, which told the story of Adam and Eve. It was performed on December 24th.

The centerpiece of the play was a vivid green fir tree adorned with shiny red apples. The colors red and green soon came to represent the colors of the Christmas season.

Over time other decorations were added, and the Paradise tree evolved into the Christmas tree.

Two legends from the sixteenth century lay claim to the
first decorated Christmas tree. One tells of an evergreen tree
trimmed with flowers that was displayed in Riga, Latvia.
Today a plaque in the town square reads, "The First New
Year's Tree in Riga 1510." In much of eastern Europe, a
Christmas Tree and a New Year's Tree were one and the same.

A second story tells of the famous German preacher, Martin Luther. While walking home one night, Luther was awed by the beauty of stars shining between the branches of a fir tree. He wanted to share this beautiful sight with his children, so he brought home a fir tree and decorated it with candles. The little flames looked like twinkling stars.

No one knows if these stories are true, but by the 1600s decorations and candles became a popular way to trim a tree. Buckets of water and sand stood nearby in case of fire.

In the 1600s Germans decorated Christmas trees with fruits and nuts. Before long, ginger cookies shaped like bells, angels, and stars were added. Tinsel made from real silver gave the tree sparkle. Sometimes books and small toys were hidden among the tree's branches, while larger gifts were placed under the tree.

German settlers brought the Christmas tree tradition to America, but not everyone welcomed it. Puritans and other religious groups banned the Christmas tree custom because of its non-Christian origins. For the same reason, in May 1659 the General Court of Massachusetts banned Christmas. It wasn't until 1856 that Christmas was made a legal holiday in Massachusetts.

On June 25, 1870, Christmas became a national holiday in the United States. American children made long strings of popcorn and cranberries, which they wound around the tree. Finely woven baskets containing tiny gifts were tucked between the branches.

In the late 1800s, Americans became fascinated with glass-blown ornaments that were arriving from Europe. To make these novel creations, craftsmen placed molten glass on the end of a blowpipe. As they blew through the pipe, the soft glass expanded and was molded into one of more than five thousand possible shapes! Around the same time, beautiful angels and glittering stars became stylish tree toppers.

In 1889 President Benjamin Harrison and his family
decorated the first White House Christmas tree.
Six years later, First Lady Frances Cleveland added
electric lights to what she called a "Technology Tree."

In 1929 First Lady Lou Henry Hoover announced
that decorating a White House tree would be an annual
affair. In the years that followed, the project became the
responsibility of each First Lady.

First Lady Jacqueline Kennedy began a tradition of themed trees. In 1961 her first tree was based on the popular Christmas ballet *Nutcracker Suite*. First Lady Betty Ford decorated with homemade tree trimmings to encourage thrift and recycling.

In recent years First Ladies have asked American artists and craftspeople to create ornaments for the White House Christmas tree. Simple or fancy, the trees reflect each First Lady's heartfelt design.

Over the years, brighter lights were developed.
They were safer, too. Now many people use energy-saving
LED lights, and a few of the nation's largest trees
are powered by solar energy.

Christmas tree lights 1903

Christmas tree lights 1930

Christmas tree lights 1947

Christmas tree lights 2009

The beloved Christmas tree has evolved, too. In the 1800s feather trees became popular, followed by trees made of aluminum or plastic, as well as artificial trees with lights already draping their branches. Despite these creative options, traditional fir trees are still preferred by many.

Feather Christmas tree from 1800s

Pink plastic Christmas tree from 1960s

Aluminum Christmas tree from 1960s

Pre-lit Christmas tree from 2009

Fir trees become Christmas trees when their graceful branches are draped with twinkling bulbs and colorful ornaments. But finding perfect trees to decorate is not always easy.

The life of a Christmas tree starts in a tree nursery, where seeds are planted in mounded soil called raised beds. After about two years the best sprouts are replanted in transplant beds, where they continue to grow. When the little trees are seven to fifteen inches (twenty to forty centimeters) tall, they are called seedlings.

A Christmas tree farmer buys seedlings from a tree nursery. Because each seedling has its own soil, nutrient, and water needs, the farmer buys varieties that will grow well in the type of soil and weather conditions found on his or her farm.

The farmer must also consider the kind of tree that people will want years in the future. Some fir trees need to grow for six to ten years before they are big enough to harvest.

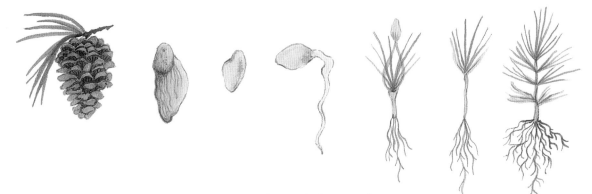

Progression of growth from seed to tree

Most Christmas trees are firs, or cone-bearing trees.
There are many different kinds of firs for people to choose.

Scotch Pine

This fir, a native of Europe and Asia, is now grown
mainly for use as a Christmas tree. Scotch pines can
be found on tree farms in the eastern United States
and Canada. Their stiff branches will hold heavy
ornaments. Scotch pines also hold their needles
better than other species.

Douglas Fir

These cold-weather trees grow from central California
to Alaska. This is the most popular Christmas tree
choice in the Pacific Northwest. Douglas fir branches
droop down, and their needles are a soft dark green.

Fraser Fir

These southern balsams are grown mostly in North
Carolina. Their neat shape, strong branches, and lovely
fragrance make them a favorite choice. Sadly, a
wingless insect called the balsam woolly adelgid is
attacking this beautiful species. Scientists are working
hard to save Frasers by controlling this tree killer.

Balsam Fir

Balsam firs grow from Pennsylvania to Canada. Their gray bark has many small blisters filled with fragrant, sticky goo called resin. To avoid sticky hands, people tend to wear gloves when handling these trees.

Eastern White Pine

The eastern white pine is the state tree of both Maine and Michigan. Its extra-long needles range in color from bluish to silver green. These trees must be trimmed regularly to keep them compact. The white pine weevil is a threat to the future of this species.

Colorado Blue Spruce

The blue spruce is the state tree of Colorado and Utah. These trees are prized for their unique blue color and their sturdy branches, which can hold heavy ornaments without sagging. Blue spruces can live for up to eight hundred years, so they are often used as living trees and are replanted after the season.

Seedlings are planted in the spring. Today, hand planting is rare. Instead, large tree farms use special machines that can plant up to twenty thousand seedlings a day! The machines' perfect spacing helps trees grow in a more uniform shape.

Despite the appeal of growing Christmas trees, these farmers face many challenges. Weather, molds, insects, and animals can cause lots of headaches. Plus, there is always the possibility of a forest fire.

One challenge farmers can't control is weather. Winter storms can be devastating. Heavy ice can cause tree branches to crack, ruining the shapes of the trees. Too much rain can cause damaging fungi and molds to grow. These can attack tree roots, needles, and trunks. Plants sick with fungus are cut down in order to save nearby trees.

woolly adelgid

aphids

Hungry insects such as aphids, budworms, grubs, mites, and the woolly adelgid weaken trees. In addition to chewing bark and needles, insects can infect trees with diseases.

Tree farmers inspect their trees throughout the growing season. When insects and their nests are found, the infested trees are cut down and destroyed. This may save other trees from infestation.

Farmers usually try to avoid using insecticides. Chemicals are expensive and unhealthy. One exception is a government rule that requires the spraying of trees going to other states. These sprays are used to stop the spread of destructive insects to other parts of the country.

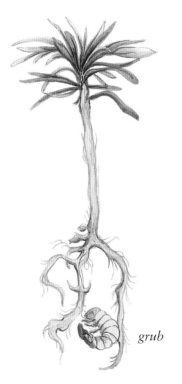

white pine weevil

grub

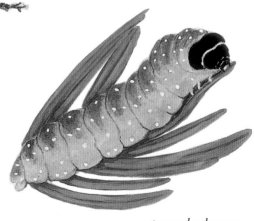

spruce budworm

Animals often cause significant tree damage.
Deer, moose, and elk trample seedlings with their hooves
and crush branches by rubbing up against them. Rodents,
such as meadow voles, chew on a layer of bark called the
cambium. This can kill a healthy tree. And because voles live
underground, the trees' roots are not spared either. Finally, rabbits
snack on new growth, slowing the trees' development.

For damage control, workers clear grass from under trees.
Despite these precautions, destructive animal behaviors will still kill
many trees before harvest.

Farmers prune tree branches that are damaged, diseased, or broken. Removing these branches keeps trees healthy. They also shave branch tips so the trees grow in perfect Christmas tree shapes.

At harvest time, trees are cut and tagged for size. Then, in a process called baling, branches are pressed to their trunks with net or string. Baling protects the trees while they're being transported. In mid-November thousands of trees are loaded into trucks and delivered to retailers.

It takes farmers years of hard work and lots of patience as
seedlings grow into mature firs. But for children the thrill of
buying a tree is immediate. With great care they choose their
trees and take them home to trim. These are magical moments,
when fir trees of all shapes and sizes become glittering Christmas
trees. Around the world people joyfully celebrate their own
special traditions, and each of their Christmas trees is unique.
Yet trimming a tree represents a happy moment in time that
brings us together as a community in an ever-changing world.

Fun Facts

 During the Revolutionary War, German and British soldiers partied around a decorated tree. It's said that the celebration provided the distraction that allowed George Washington to cross the Delaware River unnoticed and then defeat the surprised soldiers.

 In 1882 Edward Johnson, a lab assistant for Thomas Edison, assembled the first string of Christmas tree lights.

 In 1912 President Teddy Roosevelt, an environmentalist, banned Christmas trees from the White House. In an embarrassing twist, his nephews hid a tree in a closet, bringing it out on Christmas Eve.

 In 1923 President Calvin Coolidge began the tradition of a tree-lighting ceremony on the White House Lawn.

 Since 1923 a giant Christmas tree has been displayed annually in New York's Rockefeller Center. Following a year-long search by helicopter and by foot, a 75- to 90-foot Norway spruce is selected for the honor.

 According to *Guinness World Records*, the record for the tallest cut Christmas tree goes to a 221-foot Douglas fir that was displayed in 1950 at the Northgate Shopping Center in Seattle, Washington.

 The United States has more than 21,000 Christmas tree farms, which employ over 100,000 workers. More than 500,000 acres of land are planted with future Christmas trees.

Resources

Lankford, Mary D. *Christmas USA*. New York: HarperCollins, 2006.

National Christmas Tree Association
www.christmastree.org
Games and tree trivia, along with lots of useful information, make this an entertaining and instructive site.

Purmell, Ann. *Christmas Tree Farm*. New York: Holiday House, 2006.

Trapani, Iza. *Jingle Bells*. Watertown, MA: Charlesbridge Publishing, 2007.

*To my mother, whose creativity, generosity,
and fun-loving spirit made every Christmas special
—J. F.*

*To my daughters Elizabeth and Mary,
who know how to choose the prettiest Christmas tree
—J. F.*

Published by Charlesbridge
85 Main Street
Watertown, MA 02472
(617) 926-0329
www.charlesbridge.com

Library of Congress Cataloging-in-Publication Data
Farmer, Jacqueline.
   O Christmas tree : its history and holiday traditions /
Jacqueline Farmer; Illustrated by Joanne Friar.
      p. cm.
   ISBN 978-1-58089-238-4 (reinforced for library use)
   ISBN 978-1-58089-239-1 (softcover)
1. Christmas trees—History—Juvenile literature. 2. Christmas
trees—Juvenile literature. I. Friar, Joanne H. II. Title.
GT4989.F37 2010
394.2663—dc22   2009027788

Printed in China
(hc) 10 9 8 7 6 5 4 3 2 1
(sc) 10 9 8 7 6 5 4 3 2 1

Illustrations done with Holbein gouache on Fabriano Artistico hot-press watercolor paper
Display type and text type set in Letterhead Fancy and Sabon
Color separations by Chroma Graphics, Singapore
Printed and bound February 2010 by Jade Productions in Heyuan, Guangdong, China
Production supervision by Brian G. Walker
Designed by Diane M. Earley